Teacher's Friend ⁓es

I Want
Promotic

Chris Fenton

Teacher's Friend – I Want A Promotion!

Chris Fenton

Design and typesetting Fakenham Photosetting
Cover Brian Melville and Roger Penwill
Editorial Commissioned by Lucy Melville; Edited by Teresa Adams
Illustrations Roger Penwill

LCP • Hampton House • Longfield Road • Leamington Spa • Warwickshire • CV31 1XB
tel: 01926 886914 **fax:** 01926 887136
e-mail: mail@LCP.co.uk **website:** www.LCP.co.uk

ISBN 978-1-905827-85-5

Contents

Section 3: The next step

Introduction

promotion

– noun

1. advancement in rank or position.

2. furtherance or encouragement.

3. the act of promoting.

4. the state of being promoted.

5. something devised to publicize or advertise a product, cause, institution, etc., as a brochure, free sample, poster, television or radio commercial, or personal appearance.

6. Also called queening. *Chess* . the replacement of a pawn that has reached the enemy's first rank by a more powerful piece of the same color, usually a queen.

Random House Dictionary, © Random House, Inc. 2010.

Looking at the above definitions of the word 'promotion', they all seem to hit the mark, except the last, although in some respects, this definition hits the mark too. By seeking out a promotion, you have, invariably, moved forward as far as you can, by using and, ultimately, mastering all of the tools around you so far, or, as in the pawn's case, you have gone as far as you can without increasing your rank.

So, exactly how far have you moved forward in your career, and why does all of this forward movement warrant a change of status or working patterns? There is a wide variety of promotion available to teachers at varying times in their careers, but the trick to moving forward successfully is to understand exactly where you are, what you have achieved so far and then to work out how all of this experience is going to benefit you and your school in the future. For example, if you have successfully led a team of teachers or a department, set challenges for them, implemented changes and reported back on progress with evidence to your senior managers and governors, you are probably ready to enter the world of senior school management via the role of assistant or deputy headteacher. Alternatively, you may have completed two or three years of successful classroom teaching and management of some foundation subjects and can feel the first rumblings of the promotion hunger in your belly. No matter where you are in your career and no matter what your successes are and understanding of the role you have, planning for your promotion will be the single most important key to your future success.

In any profession, the psychology of seeking out a promotion is the same. Any such desire is born of one of two principles: a) the association of inflated status with overall feelings of self-worth, or b) the association of promotion with an innate desire to conquer the world around us! Either way, whether you wish to conquer the known world of education with your dazzling and previously unseen understanding of subject management, or whether you wish to bring out the inner Gandhi in you by taking on the leadership of the failing school in the inner city and liberating the staff and children from the evil tyrant of a poor education, seeking out a promotion has undertones that can leave you jaded and professionally compromised. Scary stuff then, but less so if you approach it with a level head and a broad understanding of why you want a promotion in the first place.

Aspiration is a good thing and, in fact, it is the main driving force that has led to some of the world's greatest achievements.

However, every journey begins with a first step and considering every aspect of the process itself will make the journey easier to handle and less fraught with the potential downfalls that job candidates who were less prepared have had to suffer over the years.

How to use this book

This book will not answer the interview questions for you, write your letters of application or source the perfect job for you, but what it will do is guide you through the process in a calm, orderly fashion so nobody gets hurt. It is rare for anyone seeking out a promotion to get the job they want first time. Sometimes when you get that phone call of rejection, you may want to give up altogether, since you know that you have given your all, only to end up with nothing to show for it except a smart new suit and a nagging thought that you shouldn't have tried in the first place, and 'Oh dear!, What were you thinking?'.

I Want A Promotion will help you to deal with your doubts and demons, and enable you to go for promotions in the knowledge that you have researched and prepared yourself fully. This way, no matter what the outcome of the dreaded application process, you can be confident that you have done your best and can go on to further and greater achievements in the future.

In my experience, I have applied for countless jobs, some successfully and others less so. Similarly, I have interviewed a wealth of potential candidates, giving me the opportunity to meet and work with some of the most inspiring people you can imagine. Sitting on both sides of the interviewing panel has given me the luxury of knowing how best to prepare and present yourself for the gruelling process of applying for a promotion and it is this level of experience that *I Want A Promotion* is based upon.

An important thing to remember when embarking on this journey is that people are successful and unsuccessful for a reason. Sometimes, choosing a successful candidate can be an extremely difficult process that can be deliberated for hours and, at other times, it is as simple as toast, with one candidate standing out head and shoulders above the rest. One thing for certain is that when you advertise a position, you never know who is going to apply and, to me, that is what makes the process so invigorating.

I believe that all candidates need to be celebrated for their bravery, as it takes a lot of courage to share information about yourself with complete strangers and, as we have already assessed, when there is only one job and ten potential candidates, there are going to be nine disappointed people at the end of the day, so applying for a promotion is always going to be a gamble. *I Want A Promotion*, however, is one way of reducing the risk you are about to take; it is easy to read, taking as much stress out of the process as possible. So, good luck and let the conquest begin!

Section 1: Getting started

Your career so far – an analysis of promotional readiness

A rough guide to promotions

The most important question: Why?

Getting it right from the start – playing to your strengths

Looking at it from both sides

A couple more tips before you start

The roller coaster ahead – scream if you want to get off!

So in a nutshell…

Your career so far – an analysis of promotional readiness

So, how has it been for you? So far, so good? I would imagine you have come a long way since you first opened the door of your new classroom and saw your whole first year ahead of you. Do you remember how you felt then when you were about to set sail on totally unchartered waters, full of optimism and buzz? Presumably since that first morning, you have learnt an awful lot about the world of teaching and what it encompasses, and maybe you have had some management experience as well, so much so that you feel ready to take on a new challenge. If you are now thinking about applying for a promotion, then everything should be going relatively well. But are you ready? Really ready?

Ask yourself this question and then ask it again. Before you even start, you need to feel completely ready to take on the process of job applications, because if you can't commit to the time involved then you are already at a disadvantage. Similarly, are you professionally ready to take on a new and daunting role? You may think that two years of teaching qualifies you to apply for a headship, but it is doubtful that anyone else will! You need to be realistic in your aspirations and recognise that every step forward is one step closer to your overall dream job, whatever that may be. Bypassing important professional development roles is not advisable and certainly won't make future promotions any easier. You need to think of your career progression in the same terms as a child's progression through a school. Every promotion you get throughout your career will equip you with the skills you need to make the next promotion available to you, just like what is learned in one year will help a child to access the following year's learning.

To get your first teaching job and other promotions you may have experienced so far, you will have had first-hand experience of the application and interview process for yourself. Although you may have tried to block the horror of it from your memory, the fact is that you are relatively experienced in these matters and whether you got your job first time or it took you ten attempts, every time you start the process you take something away from it.

So, whilst taking a look at your career so far, a good place to start is to write a list of your achievements to date and then prioritise them in order of relevance for the job you are thinking of applying for. Think back to the variety of experiences you have had and how, as what you took from them can be related to the promotion you want to apply for. Once you have analysed and written down the obvious ones, move on to some of the more obscure ones that can be related as well. Before you even consider taking your application further, you have now got a list of achievements that can be related to the job description you will receive (should you feel confident enough in your list to send off for the application pack in the first place!).

Experience is relative and there are many applications that are strong in some areas but not in others. Thinking about everything you have achieved and reflecting on the type of teacher you are, as well as the circumstances in which you work best, will enhance your application significantly. We will look at writing application letters in Section 2, but at the moment you need to decide whether a promotion is the right thing to go for right now and similarly whether you feel you have the skills you will need, should you get the job in the future.

So, before applying, consider the following:

1. Time: Do you have enough time to devote yourself to the application process? Remember that this will involve trawling job sites, visiting schools, planning out and writing applications, attending and preparing for interviews.

2. Experience: Are your career experiences so far relevant to the level of promotion to which you are aspiring? If not, what can you do about it?

3. Lifestyle: How will a promotion impact on your lifestyle, for example, will an increase in meetings affect your childcare or travelling arrangements?

Now that you've thought about it a little more, are you ready? If so, let's go!

A rough guide to promotions

There are a variety of different promotions available to teachers, depending on your experiences and aspirations. Some of them are internal such as becoming an Advanced Skills Teacher (AST), while others are external and usually involve leaving one school to start work at another. Whichever the promotion, the basic protocols are the same but before we go into those, the following breakdown should help you to recognise the types of promotions available to you and should go some way to helping you to focus your thoughts, relate your experiences and begin gathering the evidence needed to support your application.

Internal promotions

Internal promotions will periodically come up as your school develops. For example, as staff move on to new positions and leave the school, they leave behind a position which will, ultimately, need to be filled. When this happens, headteachers can often use it as an opportunity to reshape their staffing structure. You may be a more experienced teacher who can step up to a role that includes management responsibilities and, as such, may be invited to apply for the role. This will leave the way clear for the headteacher to employ a newly-qualified teacher (NQT) or less experienced teacher to fill the post of the person leaving. Should you find yourself in this position, the golden rule is never assume that the job is yours. No matter how well you know the school, the headteacher and the movement of the school, this is still a job application and therefore should be considered with the same amount of professionalism as an external promotion where you know nothing about the school or staff with which you hope to work.

On many occasions I have seen staff, when going for internal promotions, fall into the familiarity trap and leave themselves

wanting when asked pivotal questions at interview. Remember that the headteacher, governors and occasionally the Local Education Authority (LEA) need to be confident in your abilities to lead and manage. As a result, everything that you do throughout the process needs to emanate confidence and professionalism in order for those around you to feel confident in you and your abilities.

Newly-created internal roles

Your headteacher and management team may want to develop certain areas of the school as a result of either their self-assessment of overall school performance or the opinions of external moderators such as Ofsted. Whatever the reasons for the job creation, the leadership team will be looking internally to promote from their current team, and rewards such as Teaching and Learning Recruitment Points (TLRs) will, no doubt, be on offer. TLRs are a means of increasing pay for a specific time to ensure that a designated and specific task is implemented, measurable and ultimately achieved. Very often TLRs will be related to your performance management targets and if that is the case, then it needs to be seen as an opportunity to rise to the challenge in full consultation with your headteacher. Internal promotions such as these can be an excellent means of testing the middle management waters for your future professional development and can lead to new and exciting perspectives on your profession. Roles such as these, particularly if they include a salary increase, will undoubtedly be related to the overall raising of standards in the school and whilst you may find that brings pressure and is daunting, you need to view it as a positive pressure that can bring out qualities in you that you may not know you have.

Once again, however, applying for these internal promotions needs to be given the same amount of gravity as any other form of application.

Non-incremental internal promotions

As a second or third year teacher you will, invariably, be given the opportunity to lead a foundation subject or small project within the school as a means of developing you professionally and increasing your overall contribution to the school. Once again, if you do have to apply for these opportunities, you need to approach them with professional integrity. Usually this form of internal promotion doesn't impact on salary and, as such, will involve a chat and a lot of support. There are standard expectations of subject coordinators. A whole-school understanding of the deliverance of the subject as well as a consideration of how to move it forward are a large part of the role.

Advanced Skills Teacher status

In order to become an Advanced Skills Teacher, you need to download an application pack which, once completed, needs to be approved and forwarded by your headteacher. Once the application has been received, an assessor will visit your school to observe you teach, to interview you and to seek further approval from your headteacher and management team. If approved, you can expect to see an increase in your annual salary by between £5000 and £10,000, yet there are certain caveats you will have to follow. These include outreach work at other schools who may need support. In addition, you may have to lead workshops and deliver INSET to both internal and external staff. However, if you wish to remain in the classroom and experience similar salaries to senior managers without the desk/paperwork, then this could be the perfect route for you.

In order to be classed as an Advanced Skills Teacher, you need to deliver consistently outstanding lessons and, along with that, be able to show that your teaching is consistently impacting on the learning of children and the development of other colleagues. Similarly, your school needs to have the financial capability to be able to support an internal application. Once you have been assessed as an AST, you can use it to apply for external positions as well. You would imagine that most ASTs are extremely experienced, however, this is not always the case. ASTs come in all shapes and sizes with some being awarded the status after just three years in the profession. Becoming an AST is not about years in the job, it is about the ability to do the job, and do it well.

Crossing the pay threshold

The threshold can be crossed by teachers on point M6 of the pay system who adhere to an application process. Teachers who successfully cross the pay threshold are placed on point one of a three-point threshold pay scale. The application form asks those who wish to move forward with this form of internal promotion to demonstrate how they feel they meet the designated criteria and how they contribute to the overall development of the school.

The four threshold standards that need to be demonstrated are:

- standard 1 – core values, understanding of the curriculum and professional knowledge

- standard 2 – teaching and assessment of learning

- standard 3 – contribution to raising standards through pupil achievement

- standard 4 – effective professional development.

Applications for crossing the pay threshold are internally assessed by the headteacher who will then recommend that the application be approved. Once again, it should never be assumed that this is an automatic process. Applications will need to be evidence-based and backed up where appropriate. If an application is refused, then the reasons need to be stated. This provides an opportunity for a professional discussion which then leads to overall professional development to ensure that the application will be stronger during the next round.

External promotions

Most of the above promotions are also applicable to external applications, but should your school not be in a position to offer any form of promotion at all, then you will need to look externally. The types of jobs you will find will vary enormously, but just as your own school may be having a cabinet reshuffle leading to new opportunities, other schools may find themselves in the same position. However, if there aren't any up-and-coming applicants within the school, an open advertisement may be appropriate, leaving the door open for you or anyone who so desires to make an application for the job.

Main-scale promotions/TLR promotions

Main-scale teaching promotions will usually be offered on a full-time basis and, where appropriate, will be advertised with the appropriate TLR points and the criteria within which they are being awarded. The school will advertise the designated class or Key Stage and will highlight the professional standards required within the application pack. These external promotions are usually the first step to moving up the teaching career ladder and if you are choosing to apply for such a promotion, you will need to demonstrate an understanding of subject leadership and experience of developing both the achievements of children and the working practice of colleagues.

Head of Key Stage or department

These external promotions will require an acute understanding of the workings of the designated Key Stage or department. They will be advertised with some key characteristics and, on receipt of the application pack, you will normally find a more detailed person specification and job description which will highlight the areas within the Key Stage that need to be developed and the areas of expertise desired.

To apply confidently for a position such as this, you will need to demonstrate that you have an understanding of consultative working practice and that you have experience of leadership that has had a significant impact on standards in your school. These promotions will usually place you in the middle management team, since your work, ideas and experience will contribute to future direction of the school, all of which will be highlighted in the advertisement and the application pack.

Assistant headteacher

This is a senior management role and although it will usually carry a teaching responsibility, you will normally have designated management time for you to complete your management role. This role is normally placed on the Leadership Scale and will carry with it some whole-school responsibilities. It will be advertised as such, outlining the main roles and responsibilities, and also the essential experience required. The application pack will include further details of the defined management roles and also the teaching expectations. Like the role of a deputy headteacher, the role of an assistant headteacher is akin to spinning plates. As a member of the senior management team (SMT), you will be expected to contribute to decisions that affect the whole school and, as a member of the teaching team, you will be expected to implement them. Be sure you can demonstrate an ability to do both before proceeding with an application.

Deputy headteacher

Since you will have overall responsibility for the school at times and be playing a significant role in the leadership and direction of the school, you will need to demonstrate a very clear understanding of what constitutes good leadership and outstanding provision within a school. The initial advertisement for these positions will usually highlight the areas of expertise required, but the application pack will highlight it in more significant detail. Consider what your current deputy headteacher's role is within the school and decide whether you can match it. You will have to be seen to be a beacon of good practice at every turn and, as a result, will need to demonstrate excellent time-management, understanding, vision and ability. Some say this is the most difficult role in a school and although

I can think of others that are just as challenging for different reasons, I have to concur that as a deputy headteacher it can be advisable to keep a camp bed in your classroom!

Headteacher

If you feel ready to apply for the position of headteacher, then you will no doubt be extremely well versed in the protocols, dilemmas and hoops that you will have to jump through in order to land the 'big job'. Needless to say, you have to be able to demonstrate experience, understanding, vision and authority throughout the application process. Applying for a headship is a tough process – some may say tougher than the job itself. Make your own mind up about that one, but regardless of the position, you will still need to decide whether you are ready and then commit the same amount of time, dedication and professionalism to the application process as if you were applying for your first promotion. You may have to get more across, but you still need to do it in the same way.

So, there you go. These are just some of the types of external and internal promotions available to you, each carrying their own responsibilities and routines, but all exactly the same in terms of process. Some of them will require you to demonstrate your teaching, some will require you to give a presentation, some will call on you to complete a range of tasks and others will require you to do all of these and more. No matter what the position, before you apply, you need to decide if you are ready and if you are, then you need to brace yourself, because sometimes applying for a promotion isn't pretty and can leave you dazed, confused and slightly sweaty. It's worth it though because eventually after all those sleepless nights, dry mouths and kick-yourself moments, it all comes together and you get the call to tell you you've got the job. Brilliant!

The most important question: Why?

It may sound stupid, but it really is an important question to ask before you even start putting the promotion feelers out there – why do you want a promotion? Nobody in their right mind would put themselves through the gruelling agony that applying for a job can sometimes be without really wanting it, right? Well, in my experience, the reasons that people apply for promotions vary greatly, and sometimes the reason can be patently obvious when you meet at interview and ask a few leading questions.

Most of the time, people are genuinely ready and feel that even though they are very happy at their current school, there simply aren't any opportunities for them to grow professionally and that, in itself, is stifling them. The references you receive will usually back this up and here is an important question that you need to be asking yourself before you begin the process – what will my reference say about me? We will address this later, but the earlier you start to think about this the better.

So, why do you want to be promoted? What is your mindset and what is it that makes you feel that you will be successful? I am not urging you to consider this to be negative or to hold you back in any way. Instead, I wish to encourage you to ensure you are doing it for the right reasons. In some cases, a sideways move might be a better consideration. You will still have to go through the rigmarole of applying, but if you are unhappy at your current school, for whatever reason, jumping to the conclusion that a promotion is the right way forward may well be the wrong decision in this case. If you aren't professionally equipped for a promotion then you will put a lot of effort into what potentially will be a fruitless and exasperating exercise.

The next thing to be aware of is the promotional hunger. You will have been successful so far and may be feeling that you can do anything, so why shouldn't you go for the next step up, even if it is a little early in your career to be considering it? Well, if that is how you are feeling then go for it, but before you do, think about the person on the other end of the application form. If they look at your application form and see glaring gaps in experience, no matter how well you have tried to hide them, then they are highly unlikely to invite you for interview. Again, consider what you have achieved so far before putting finger to keyboard, because if you can't walk the walk at interview, it will be very obvious and will leave you frustrated. Very often applying for promotions is as much about being in the right place at the right time as it is about being well prepared and putting on a good performance at the interview. The promotion hunger monster is a dangerous beast and will leave you feeling empty. So before you choose to punch above your weight, think carefully about whether your application will be taken seriously and plan accordingly.

Another common reason for applying for promotions is that you may feel undervalued at work and feel that you can do so much more. There may be a reason why you haven't been given the opportunities you crave so much, and a frank discussion with your headteacher or SMT might clear the air and raise issues of which you were not initially aware. Once you are armed with this information, you can begin to do something about it. Remember that starting at a new school isn't easy, particularly if you have a new-found authority amongst your colleagues. If you aren't ready for a promotion, other more experienced staff members may see it much more quickly than you do, so a professional conversation about your aspirations shouldn't be a negative experience if you are feeling undervalued.

Whatever your reasons for seeking out a promotion, consider them carefully because they may offer you a deeper insight into yourself and your professional standing than you initially thought. This can be very empowering and will make the process of plotting out the future in preparation for a promotion.

Getting it right from the start – playing to your strengths

OK, so you've considered whether you are ready to seek out a promotion, the type of promotion you are ready to go for and your reasons for going for it. You are now in a position to get yourself organised in a way that enables all of your previous experiences and current roles/responsibilities to be made relevant to the position you want to go for. Start this process by building your experience log.

This needs to be a positive and reflective journal that highlights your successes in the classroom and as a member of the school team (quantifying them where possible). Think hard because sometimes some of the most innocuous events from your career can show an understanding of a principle or exemplify how you have helped the school to achieve a goal.

For example:

'organised and directed the school play'

may seem a relatively unimportant part of your role, but if it is emphasised in the following way, then it starts to take on more significance:

'contributed to the school's community cohesion agenda through directing and organising the school play. This facilitated children's social skills and sense of personal development, and cohesively linked the curriculum to further learning.'

By listing your achievements first and then relating them to the wider educational agenda, you will start to build up a personal profile that makes total use of your experiences so far and begins to put them into the right context.

The next job is to seek out advice from a person in the school who is currently doing the job that you wish to be promoted to. Ask your headteacher if you can shadow that staff member or at least spend some time with them to go through their role and begin to build a clear understanding of what the role entails. When you begin the application process, this will be an incredible help since it will show that you have a broad understanding of the role. But perhaps most importantly, you will begin to relate the main competencies of the job you are aiming for to your current role, drawing similarities, allowing you to show on your application form and at interview that you understand the role and will be able to accomplish it since you have experience of some of the main competencies in your current role. Seeking out similarities between the job you do and the one that you want to do will help you to focus yourself and apply for positions with confidence. Similarly, there may be areas in which your experience is lacking and, as a result, you can begin to identify ways in which you can develop them.

Finally, begin to consider the type of school you would like to work in. If you work in a two- or three-form entry school then you might feel stifled in a one-form entry school. Alternatively, if you are used to a one-form entry school, will you be overwhelmed in a larger school, particularly if you have a new position of authority? Where would you like your new school to be? Are you used to working in the inner city or in the suburbs, and, therefore, where would you feel most comfortable? It is important to mention that if you want to progress to more senior roles in education, then a variety of different schools on your CV will help you to stand out. However, if this is your first promotion, you need to consider where it is going to be most comfortable for you to complete a good job, enabling you to grow in confidence as you develop professionally.

Looking at the process of applying for a promotion in this measured manner will reduce the chances of you feeling out of your depth when it comes to applying and even starting the role. School positions tend to come in waves, giving time for resignations to run their course. If you begin to look through advertisements, you will see that positions advertised early in the autumn term usually expect new appointees to start at the beginning of the following term and so on. This will give you time to begin plotting your course of action. If you start looking at your career so far in September and begin planning out how to embellish your experiences and grow in understanding of the role you require throughout the autumn term, when the spring term begins, you will be further equipped to begin the process. Then, over the next two terms will find yourself applying for and, hopefully, attaining your promotion in time for the next autumn term to begin. It isn't a sprint, nor is it a walk in the park; applying for promotions in a way that increases your chances of success can be lengthy, but that doesn't mean it needs to be frustrating. By considering your career so far, how you would like it to progress, the ins and outs of the job you are aspiring to and how best to gain the appropriate experiences, you are placing yourself in a much stronger position to be successful during the application process and, more importantly, to do a good job in the future.

Looking at it from both sides

No matter what the position you aspire to, the application form you send, the observed lesson that you teach and the interview that you give will all be received and assessed by the other part of the promotion equation, namely, the people who are either going to offer you the position or reject you. What this basically means is that everything you do from the moment you send off your application to the moment you say your goodbyes and leave the interview room, is going to be viewed and assessed by a third party. That's why it is so very important that you have done your homework and enhanced your understanding of the job in hand before you make an application.

Make no mistake, the headteacher will know exactly the type of experience that they feel to be important to do the job, and they will also be able to see through any attempt to make up for a lack of experience or preparation. So, it seems obvious that when writing your letter of application or considering your answers at interview, you should bear this in mind. The way to be confident that you are speaking the same language as the headteacher and interview panel is to have investigated thoroughly. A great deal of information can be honed from the application pack you will receive. Your application pack will usually include a letter of introduction from the chair of governors or the headteacher, a school prospectus, an application form, a job description, a person specification, some attainment results, and usually an Ofsted report. It is these last four pieces of information that will give you the best background knowledge. By analysing them thoroughly, you will pick out clear words and phrases that will help you to begin building a profile of what the appointment team will be looking for. For example, if the job description calls for a clear understanding of national policies, you can quite confidently assume that the headteacher needs someone who can keep abreast of changes as they happen and is able to relay information coherently to staff. Similarly, if the person specification expects the successful candidate to have a strong command of a variety of classroom management techniques, you can make an educated guess that discipline could be an issue in either the class you will be expected to teach or possibly even the whole school. As obvious as these may seem and as mandatory as they may be to the job, there are often very clear reasons for highlighting them in the application pack.

The Ofsted report will also give you an idea of how well the school is doing and this, in itself, will you give you a wealth of ammunition from which you can begin building your responses, both in your application form and interview. For example, the report may state that teaching and learning in Key Stage 2 is less adequate than in Key Stage 1. This will mean, of course, that the headteacher is hoping to strengthen the Key Stage 2 team by employing a strong teacher who can lead the work of others. This is now an opportunity to demonstrate, at every level possible, that you can do just that, based on your experiences so far and your understanding of the job description.

It is also a good idea to read previous reports as well so you can gauge where and how the school has improved the most. This is now your chance to apply your experience to the areas that the school is doing well in, illustrating that you can complement the work already taking place, but since you have also stated that you can help to strengthen some of the areas of weakness as well, you are putting yourself in a very strong position and making yourself very appealing to the appointing panel.

Making reference to Ofsted information during your interview is a good way of showing that you have researched the school and, as such, are a thorough and well-rounded candidate. Be careful not to overstate this though as you can come across as over-keen or even glib. The headteacher already knows how well the school is or is not doing and is more interested in discovering how you will contribute to the future of the school, not how much you know about it already, however, the occasional reference will show your conscientiousness and obvious desire to be a part of the team.

Another consideration is how succinct and clear you can be when responding to the person specification in your letter of application and answering the questions at interview. To give you some trade secrets, when an appointment panel is judging whether to invite you for interview or even offer you the job, they each have an agreed checklist that highlights some of the key words and competencies they expect you to mention at each stage. As the applications are read and your answers are listened to, they will be ticking these off as you mention them. The more ticks you get, the more chance you have of progressing. (I bet you didn't see that one coming!) So, you need to be able to weed out the information required and give it as succinctly as you can when invited to do so.

If you are uncertain of what is being asked of you, it is good practice to ask more experienced colleagues to help. This way you can begin to refine your answers, ensuring they include all the information required whilst making them as concise as possible. We will look at this in more detail in Section 2, but at this stage, whilst you are considering the whole application process, it is pertinent to consider how you would feel if you were greeted with a letter of application of novel proportions. You will have to give it due consideration, but the more words you include, the less likely those in the shortlisting panel will be able to find the pertinent words and phrases. In short, make it as easy for them as possible and that way, they will be delighted when receiving a well-considered, succinct application that shows an understanding and appreciation of the process itself.

Similarly, the more direct the answer you give in response to the questions asked, the more chance there is that the panel will be able to pick out the important information without having to wade through the thick treacle of ten-minute answers. Remember, the longer you talk, the more chance you will have of going off the subject. I remember very clearly, a candidate being interviewed for a Key Stage 2 Manager position, taking fifteen minutes to answer the question that was 'Tell us a little about yourself and why you think you would make a good KS2 Manager at our school'. By the end of the fifteen minutes, she had only just finished telling us a 'little' about herself and naturally had completely forgotten the original question. She was, of course, very nervous and later apologised for her nerves, going on to give some great answers later in the interview. However, she frequently made it difficult to pick out the important information and so, consequently, was unsuccessful.

The point here is that an active consideration of the receiving party and what they are looking for will help you to focus your thinking when you start the promotion process. Once you have completed an initial letter of application, it is again good practice to have it read through by a more experienced colleague alongside the person specification to gain their view as to whether you have met all of its requirements with your answers. A bottle of wine would also be a good idea if only to persuade them a little more firmly to give you a hand!

A couple more tips before you start

We have covered quite a lot of ground so far, but there are other tips and clues that will help you to be absolutely certain you are a) experienced enough, and b) ready for the ride before you start.

1. Just to get a feel for the process, send off for some applications for jobs you would potentially like to go

for, considering everything we have covered so far, and begin to judge exactly what the school is looking for and whether you feel that you fit the mould. This is an ideal means of deciding your next steps and will certainly help you to action plan for your future. You may, for example, need some further continuous professional development in areas of management or subject specialism. You may just need management experience, full stop. To be frank, the entire person specification might be complete gobbledegook to you or there may be certain areas that you think you understand but might just need a little reassurance. Whatever issues this exercise throws up, it will be a worthwhile means of getting back into promotion shape!

2. When you are beginning to feel more confident and wish to begin applying for promotions, ask your headteacher or someone on the management team to give you an idea of some of the questions you may be expected to answer. Whilst they might not be able to give you any of the exact questions, they may be able to give you some generic questions and perhaps, most importantly, they will be able to give you some ideas of the answers you should be giving. This can prove to be an extremely profitable exercise and will serve to give you a head start. If you aren't comfortable asking your headteacher, there are a variety of websites which can offer you examples of the type of questions you may be asked, the types of answers that would help you to procure the position and, finally, an analysis of the skills that are being assessed through such questions. Remember, forewarned is forearmed!

The roller coaster ahead – scream if you want to get off!

Make no bones about it, applying for a promotion is not an easy business and no matter how many stories you hear of others just 'falling' into their dream jobs, at some point in their careers, everyone has to go for an interview. The trick is to expect it to be tough and then to do everything you can to ease the pain.

Emotionally, applying for promotions can be exhausting, therefore you will have to be as mentally prepared as you are professionally. You need to recognise that sometimes, failure is part of the process of achieving success and there may just be an occasion when you are absolutely convinced that you have got the job, only to receive a phone call that informs you of quite the opposite. You may think that there was a definite spark of professional understanding between you and the headteacher, that your answers were well considered, crackling with experience and enthusiasm and just long enough. You might be convinced that your presentation was interesting, informative and forward thinking, and it probably was. It's just that another candidate may have crackled just a little bit more or may have had just a little more experience than you in a vital area that was backed up in their answers; as a result, you were unsuccessful, but they were not. If that is the case then as hard as it is to take in after all of the effort and preparation of your application process, at some point, you will have to.

Rejection can be difficult to take. We can see it as a slight on our personality and our professionalism, but it isn't. It just means that on this occasion you were not the right person for the job and, as such, you have to trust in the judgement of the appointment panel and consider whether you actually were right at all. You may feel you were, but the people who know the school best, also know best in these situations and so long as they are in charge, their decision is final, no matter how much you want to tell the interviewers that their breath smelt and their hands were sweaty!

Whether you are successful or not, the extreme pressure that you will be under when you apply for a job and the adrenaline that it will inevitably create when you go to interview will lead to some form of downer as the adrenaline wears off. BE PREPARED FOR THIS! Try not to allow it to consume you as you begin to dissect every part of your interview, and even try to use it as a propellant to bigger and better things. This may seem patronising or even worse like a platitude, but rejection really can serve as the fuel to achieving greater things. You will need to consider why you were unsuccessful, the analysis of which will serve to help you next time around. You should receive some feedback from the headteacher about why you were unsuccessful, so when you do, make notes and be prepared to consider them carefully when you next apply. They will come in useful.

Success is also a part of the process, even though the fear of not achieving it can occasionally be debilitating. Kipling described both success and failure as 'imposters' in the classic poem *If*, and he was absolutely right. Let's put this into perspective. No matter what the odds at interview or even at the point of application, you are always battling against unknown enemies whose experience you know nothing about. Being human, it is easy to assume that everyone else who has applied is more experienced than you, has already done a similar job or, even worse, knows the chair of governors, and this sense of panic can often lead you to underperform when it most matters. Furthermore, the odds of you answering every question perfectly or your experience matching the requirements exactly are similarly low, so when it all comes down to it, when you are successful it is usually down to a combination of factors that swing in your favour when the sum total of your application is calculated. As clinical as all this sounds, all of the people called for interview will have similar qualities that the appointment panel will want to explore, so it makes sense that unless there is one outstanding candidate, a decision will be made as a result of all of your responses, meaning your chances of success are equal to your chances of failure. That said, Kipling also recommended that you 'treat both of these imposters just the same'. The man obviously hadn't been for interviews!

So, when all is considered, you are probably unhinged to even think about putting yourself through the process, but since it is the only way of getting the promotion you desire, sadly, it seems you will have to.

So, in a nutshell...

Throughout your career, if you want to move up the ranks until you are master of all you survey or even if you just want to see what life is like a little higher up the tree, you will, at some point, have to go through an ordeal called the application process. As well as considering and writing a letter of application, if you get to stage two, you will have to steel yourself for further scrutiny during the interview. To make matters worse, dependent upon the sadistic nature of the panel, you may have to give a ten-minute presentation or complete some aptitude tests or, worse still, both!

No matter what the ordeal that lies ahead of you, however, there are ways of making it less problematic and more positive, helping you to secure your dream job with as little stress as possible.

1. Pre-prepare. Find out as much about the job as possible before you apply and then begin to identify as many of the required skills and experiences that you have in your arsenal. If you haven't got enough, then figure out ways that you can get them with help from your colleagues and senior managers.

2. Consider absolutely everything that you have achieved so far in your career (no matter how small), and begin to relate it to the job description and person specification, making full use of education speak.

3. Read up on the school, ensuring that you know its context, successes and areas for development. That way you can begin to apply your experience to the school's needs, making you irresistible!

4. Accept that you may be unsuccessful but you must carry on. Remember that getting a promotion that pays more money is not going to be easy, so by accepting that failure can be a part of the process, you can use any negative experiences to your advantage.

So, just a few tips to ease you through and if you haven't been put off yet, Section 2 will dissect each part of the process and help you to find your way through the twists and turns that lie ahead.

Section 2: The application process

The application pack

Filling in the application form:

    – dos and don'ts

    – references

Writing your letter of application:

    – the short story

    – the novel

    – the pamphlet

    – slim pickings

    – so, how then?

The observed lesson:

    – teaching in a foreign environment

    – tips for teaching in a foreign environment

    – tips for teaching in your own environment

    – a final tip

The presentation

    – strategic

    – tactical

    – operational

The interview:

- presentation

- answering questions – part 1

- answering questions – part 2

- the old 'getting them to tell you what they're looking for' trick

- success and failure at interview

- feedback

So, in a nutshell…

The application pack

Once you have made the bold step to apply for a promotion, the first thing you will need to do is apply for an application pack by email, telephone or letter. Although you won't be offered the job because of anything you do at this stage, it is just common sense to ensure that any emails or hand-written letters are grammatically correct and well presented, or if telephoning a school that your manner is pleasant and professional. Remember at this stage, you don't know who will be responding to the emails, letters or telephone calls, so a good first impression is very important.

Once you receive the application pack, you can expect to find information that will tell you more about the school and occasionally the LEA in which you are applying to work. More importantly, it will tell you about the requirements of the job itself. These will manifest themselves in the following ways:

1. Information about the school – this will usually be a school brochure and will give the basic information about the school, some of its policies and its procedures.

2. Ofsted information – this is obviously a very important document and will give you an insight into the school's

current position, what their areas for development are and the areas in which they are achieving well. You will be able to gain a lot of insight into the school and the general ethos from this, so read it well. Depending on the job that is being advertised, you might also get other relevant assessment information.

3. An application form – this is usually a generic LEA form asking for general information about you, your education and the addresses, etc. of schools you have worked at previously. This will also include a section in which you can write your letter of application. Since you will wish to write more than the space provided, it is wise just to write a little note highlighting that your letter of application is included on separate sheets (just to avoid any confusion!).

4. The job description – this will outline in detail exactly what you will be expected to do in your new role. Read it well and also read between the lines to identify exactly what type of experience they are looking for.

5. The person specification – this, apart from the Ofsted information, is the most important document in the pack as far as you are concerned, because it tells exactly what you need to show to the appointment panel in your application for you to be shortlisted. Read it with a magnifying glass to ensure that you maximise every possible opportunity to highlight how you meet it, both in your letter of application and at interview, since it will be from this that the appointment panel will draw up their checklist.

Everything that you receive in this pack will help you to draw up a spotless application, so neither disregard nor overlook any part of it as all of the clues are there.

Filling in the application form

The application form is very often seen as the easy part of the process, but if you take this attitude, you are leaving yourself open to errors that might seem small but that can really stand out when the application forms are collated.

Do's and Don'ts

1. Do not lie! Make sure every little piece of information is correct because if it isn't, (and things such as previous jobs, qualifications and addresses can and very often will be checked), it will disqualify you immediately from further proceedings.

2. And again, just to reiterate, do not lie. It is the number one nail in the application coffin.

3. Do not be tempted to rush this part of the process, making mistakes that you will later need to rectify.

4. Do read carefully how the appointment team would like the form to be filled in, i.e. they might require block capitals and black ink. These are important since they show the team you have read the form and have been conscientious. Imagine how your form will look in blue if all the rest are in black; it will stand out but for the wrong reasons and may even get you disqualified.

5. Do make a couple of photocopies of the application form (using a colour photocopier if necessary), so if you do make a mistake, you can start again rather than cross out or worse, use correction fluid.

6. Do make sure your entire form is easy to understand and clearly written. I know this may seem obvious, but it will

be photocopied many times and, as such, any uncertainty over what words say will make it a more frustrating process for those involved, meaning that again, your application will stand out for the wrong reasons.

The main thing to remember about application forms is that whilst they may seem easy and straightforward, preparation is the key; it is often better to fill it in first and write a list of all the things you need to seek clarification on, such as postcodes and phone numbers of schools, exact exam qualifications and exam bodies, and that way you won't be scrabbling around at midnight looking for them the night before the application is due to be handed in. My tip about photocopying the application form has also got me out of a few scrapes in the past as well!

The final thing to consider when filling in your application form is who to include as a referee. Think carefully about this since, even though you will have to include your current headteacher or even your LEA, depending on the promotion, your other referees should be professional (unless otherwise requested) and should back up everything you have included in your application form. It is always a good idea to seek permission first, particularly from your current headteacher as this shows both good manners and professionalism. It also means that your referees will be more likely to respond quickly and appropriately, should they be asked.

So, your application form is clear, factual, honest and reflects your experience. Now for the letter of application. Brace yourself, because sometimes these are not pretty!

References

Whilst this may seem obvious since you are currently employed and, in your opinion, should be able to rely on the opinion of your headteacher, you need to be aware that headteachers talk to each other. Gone are the days of taking references on face value. Any headteacher worth their salt will check and double check references to be certain that they are not taking on a bundle of trouble that will only hinder the progression of their school rather than help it. Remember, the school is making an investment in you, as much as they are taking a gamble so they want to be sure that it is an educated gamble. Your references will be scrutinised and if anything stands out then do not be surprised if your headteacher calls you in for a chat to ask why they have just put the phone down after a thirty minute conversation with a rather disgruntled equal if you have told any slight porkies on your application form. This will do two things:

1. Strike you out of the application process immediately.

2. Endanger your current position since the headteacher will begin to feel uneasy about your reasons for wanting to leave.

To avoid such a catastrophe, be honest, truthful and think about who you will use as your referees since their overall judgement of you will play an enormous part in your progression through the application process.

Writing your letter of application

So, you are ready to make a start on one of the most time-consuming elements of the promotion process: your letter of application. The time has come to sit down with a list of all your relevant experiences to date and the person specification/job description and begin to pair them up. If you do this right, it will be the magic key that opens the route to interview, but get it wrong and it will leave you dazed, confused and frustrated.

The trick here is simplicity, succinctness and above all else, to hit all of the key points outlined in the person specification. What the appointment panel doesn't want is to have to wade through reams of reasons why you might be of interest to them. What they do want is to be able to see enough relevant experience for them to invite you to elaborate further at interview. You will not be appointed on your application form alone so it is of vital importance that you endeavour to make your letter of application tempting enough to intrigue them, leading them to implore you to tell them more.

The following categories of application letters should make all of this a little clearer and if they don't then they will, at the very least, give you some pointers on what not to do and, alternatively, what you should be aiming for.

The short story

The short story letter of application reads just like that, a short story. It has a beginning, a middle and an end, and throughout the process it takes the reader through the various ups and downs of a candidate's experiences so far with an informal tone and too much familiarity. It takes the person specification as its main plot and uses the candidate as the central character. An example of this type of letter is as follows:

The person specification has asked for the successful appointee to be

'a competent and imaginative class teacher'.

The short story writer will see this as the perfect opening and will respond appropriately. For example,

'I began teaching in autumn 2006 and from the beginning I knew it was the right profession for me. Where others had scoffed at me for wanting to take on such a challenging role, I found that my natural imagination and ability to talk to children made me stand out from other teachers my age.'

You can imagine the length of such a letter and the amount of time it would take the appointment panel to pick out the appropriate information to tick off.

Letters like these have no place in the shortlisting pool because they haven't taken the process seriously enough. A little insight into the appointment process will soon reveal that it is a very time-consuming process and headteachers and governors are extremely keen to invite the right candidates to interview so as not to lengthen the process unnecessarily. At the end of a letter like this, the appointment panel may have been entertained, but unless they can be confident in your abilities based on your experience, then they will be hard-pressed to invite someone who puts forward a short story letter for interview.

The novel

In the same vein as the short story letter, the novel is basically an overlong, exaggerated attempt to make sure that all the bases have been covered and nothing, absolutely nothing, that could be deemed worthy of inclusion has been left out. On most standard LEA application forms, it will say the following or similar:

'Use this space to add any further information about your professional experience that will complement your application'.

The novel writer will take this to mean:

'Please include every minute detail of your professional experience so far so we can scrutinise it, fall asleep halfway through it and struggle to identify which bits of experience are relevant and which aren't'.

Including too much information will, ultimately, limit your application. Even though appointment teams are duty-bound to offer interviews to anyone who can show clearly that they have met the criteria, too much information can cloud the point you are trying to make and, as a result, you may find that the appointment panel struggle to confidently identify it. For example, where a person specification calls for candidates to be able to

'manage small teams, helping them to reach challenging targets'

A novel writer will respond with an inordinate amount of detail, making it unclear whether they have actually met that part of the person specification or not. For example,

'Managing a small team takes tenacity, confidence and an approachable personality. If any of these qualities are missing, team leaders will find it difficult to maintain clarity of vision, progress towards targets or a developing sense of team work. During my time as Assessment Coordinator at St Anywhere Primary School, I built up a small team consisting of four teachers, two teaching assistants and a parent governor. During this time the school introduced a new assessment system that expected teachers to analyse their

termly assessment results and to set targets for the children in their class, based on the assessment results achieved. This was not an easy process for staff because they were unused to the system and similarly were uncertain whether it would help to raise standards at all. The system is now in place at the school and staff are more confident in its application although there is still some way to go to ensure that it is thoroughly embedded in the school.'

This response neither shows that the candidate has had successful experience of leading a small team or similarly, whether they were helped in achieving the limited goal achieved. The response is negative and can offer no quantitative evidence to suggest any practical impact that their strategies had. It takes up loads of paper though and some of the words are very big!

The pamphlet

The pamphlet is the polar opposite of the other varieties of the aforementioned application letters since it offers little information to the appointment panel, no reference to the job description and is, in fact, just a promotional exercise. It highlights in short bursts what the teacher has done and skirts around the issue of what the school is looking for by merely highlighting what has happened to them since they qualified. In essence, when an application like this is received, it falls to the appointment panel to perform a kind of guessing game, involving filling in the gaps and identifying just how exactly the candidate fits at all! This, as I'm sure you can imagine, is a tiresome exercise when faced with a pile of application forms and will render the application as defunct quite quickly.

A good tip to remember here is that appointment panels like their job to be made very easy for them. To do this, make your letter of application as explicitly referenced to the person specification as is humanly possible, drawing on every piece of experiential evidence possible to highlight how you fit.

This way, the appointment panel will have an easy job ticking the boxes necessary and inviting you for interview. Job done!

Pamphlets are usually sparse in relevant information, but abundant in flowery facts that sell the candidate in all the wrong ways. For example, when a person specification calls for the candidate to have

'a good level of core subject expertise',

a pamphlet writer may write:

'I've worked in a variety of different schools and in a variety of different settings, all of which have called on me to have an understanding of the National Curriculum. This has helped me to teach with enthusiasm and allowed me to use a wealth of resources. I always teach with enthusiasm and interest, empowering children to enjoy the curriculum and the world around them.'

Lovely, but not relevant to the question in hand. There is no emphasis on intrinsic teaching style, understanding of effective subject knowledge and, to be honest, what the core subjects actually are. This would lead me to believe that this candidate is quite arrogant and would find it difficult to manage themselves, let alone the work of others. Make your responses clear and you will score points for both understanding the requirements and showing that you are capable of meeting them.

Slim pickings

It is one thing to be concise, but it is quite another to present an application form that is sparse and leaves the appointment panel guessing whether you have the right experience to do a thorough job. Applicants who offer slim pickings will highlight that they know what the job description means, without following it up with experiences that qualify their understanding. For example, where a person specification suggests that a candidate needs to

'show good communication skills',

a writer of slim pickings may respond by stating:

'Communication is vital in schools for teams to run smoothly, management to get their ideas across competently and teachers to inspire and encourage effective learning from their pupils. Without effective communication, schools can fail to move forward as a team, leaving staff and children feeling both isolated and confused.'

Brilliant! Inspired! Never a truer word spoken, but where is the evidence from the candidate to back up how they have communicated effectively and the impact it had on standards in the school? In reality, these types of letters are a kind of smoke screen that prevent the appointment panel from seeing whether the potential candidate has the experience to make an impact at their school, leaving them guessing and making the application much more likely to fall by the wayside.

So, how then?

What should you be doing and how can you link both understanding and experience in such a way that it renders the appointment panel powerless under your spell and with absolutely no choice other than to excitedly invite you for interview to find out a little more? Well, it's not easy, but once you get into the groove of putting your answers into a format, it becomes much more straightforward.

The format we are talking about is not applied mathematics, nor is it particularly revolutionary, but it is tried and it is tested and above all else, it works.

The three key words when responding to a person specification are:

Understanding   Experience   Contribution

Any appointment worth their salt will want to see that you understand what is required and why it is important, that you have the experience to back up your understanding and that through this you have something to contribute to the future development of the school. Get these across in your letter of application and it is straight through to round two and collect £200 as you go! But be careful, it sounds easy, but it takes a little time and practice to get it just right.

As a way of helping, let us consider some of the requirements of a person specification that we have addressed earlier.

This particular school, amongst other things, is looking for

'a competent and imaginative class teacher'

and

'an ability to manage small teams, helping them to reach challenging targets'.

So, how would you respond? It might be easy for you to make a start, but before you do, you need to consider the styles mentioned earlier. The eager ones amongst you will find it easy to write a short story, novel or pamphlet, whereas those who are a little more reticent might approach these answers with a more 'slim pickings' approach. However, before you even think about attempting to start writing, let us look again at the mantra that you need to recite before putting finger to keyboard:

Understanding   Experience   Contribution

Taking the first requirement, 'a competent and imaginative class teacher', an answer that follows the mantra might look like this:

Understanding – *For a class teacher to bring the curriculum to life, they need to be able to both fully understand the requirements of the National Curriculum and build on them to ensure that teaching is accessible and relevant. Furthermore, if high quality teaching is to impact on pupils' learning, it needs to be done in an atmosphere of positive classroom management and continuous learning support.*

Experience – *Since the start of my career my thoroughness, originality and enthusiasm for learning have always been commended by school management and Ofsted inspectors alike. This has led to my teaching being defined overall as good with outstanding features and has contributed significantly to the school's improved standards.*

Contribution – *I now mentor NQTs and am continuously looking for ways to further improve my teaching. I aim to continue developing professionally, the outcomes of which will benefit all pupils and colleagues in the future.*

This is a well-rounded answer that is thorough and inviting. The appointment panel will be eager to read on. Now let us look at the second requirement, 'an ability to manage small teams, helping them to reach challenging targets':

Understanding – *A team leader needs to host a wealth of personality traits that lead to the team trusting their judgements and following their path. Professional credibility, honesty, enthusiasm and communication skills all contribute to the effective running of a small team and, in turn, will be rewarded as other team members develop professionally.*

Experience – *Whilst leading Key Stage 2, I have implemented a range of whole-school strategies in both teaching and assessment, leading to more focused, target-based learning, impacting positively on standards and on overall staff moral. My KS2 team are now confident in their own abilities and regularly contribute ideas and suggestions in meetings, based on their own positive experiences.*

Contribution – *I aim to build on my strengths as a team leader to impact on other school stakeholders and areas of whole-school development, such as community cohesion and the development of extended schooling.*

Again, this answer shows commitment and enthusiasm, leading the appointment team to be significantly more likely to invite the candidate to interview to find out some more. The key in both of these answers is that the candidate has chosen one element of their experience and matched it well to the job description. This highlights their strengths far better than trying to cram everything into the form at the appropriate time. Other questions will lend themselves to other experiences, so spread them out for maximum effect.

Basically, writing a letter of application is a detailed process, but it doesn't have to be as time-consuming as it suggests. The main objective is to give the school a flavour of your experiences and capabilities, encouraging them to interview you to find out more. Brevity without omitting the important stuff will get an appointment panel's curiosity flowing enough for them to want to know more, and that leads us to the next hurdles to your promotional dreams: the observed lesson and the interview!

The observed lesson

If you have applied for a promotion that involves a teaching responsibility, you can expect appointment panels either to invite a candidate into their school to teach the class they will prospectively be responsible for in the future, or similarly, to visit the teacher in their own environment to gain a perspective on what they currently do.

This is common practice and, to be honest, has become a mainstay of any form of appointment in the teaching world, and why not? How can you appoint someone to one of the most important professions in the world, without first checking that they can actually do it, and do it well? The simple answer is that you can't, and so you should prepare yourself for the fact that you will be observed doing what you do best. So, no matter whether your promotion involves copious amounts of teaching or not, the fact that you are guiding and informing others will, at the very least, require you to be able to deliver nothing less than a good standard of teaching with, of course, outstanding features.

So, what should you be doing to make sure that you shine throughout this process? Since this part of the appointment process falls into two camps – teaching in their school or teaching in yours – you will have to prepare appropriately for either eventuality.

Teaching in a foreign environment

To be honest, this is always a difficult exercise for all of the obvious reasons. Firstly, you don't know any of the children in the class or their nuances and you won't have any solid foundations to base your lesson on other than a verbal guide from the teacher in most cases, so this exercise needs to be treated cautiously. The teacher will have been instructed to give you as much information as possible, but you need to be aware that the appointment panel will be looking to see how you deal with this strange environment. Most good teachers will be able to handle most situations using the basics of positive behaviour management, involved and interactive teaching and learning, alongside challenging learning intentions. All of this should lead to a good learning environment and focused, keen learners. But, and it is a big but, you will be expected to deal with eventualities as they arise and a school who is looking to employ a high quality candidate will not pander to the fact that this is an alien environment with children who may be challenging. They will, in fact, openly invite candidates into these environments to assess their responses and ability to cope. Children are very perceptive and will pick up on the fact that they are involved in an unusual situation. Very often they will capitalise on it to their own amusement, so you need to be prepared to respond to any eventuality you may be faced with.

Tips for coping in a foreign environment

1. Visit the school before the lesson.

2. Ensure, first and foremost, that you are familiar with the school's behaviour management policy well before you enter the school.

3. Ensure that you have been given information regarding Special Educational Needs (SEN) and Gifted and Talented children, and plan work accordingly.

4. Ensure you know which (if any) support staff will be available to you and ensure they are clear of your expectations.

5. Ask the teacher what the children like to do and how they learn best.

6. Ask the teacher and teaching assistants for any potential hot spots for inappropriate behaviour or unusual reactions.

7. Plan a lesson that is interactive and investigative to ensure that the children are challenged and engaged.

8. Ensure you have an extension activity prepared for children who finish early (just in case you pitch the lesson too low).

9. If you are going to use ICT, make sure any resources or downloaded information is compatible with the school's systems.

10. Have a paper copy of anything stored on a memory stick that can be photocopied, just in case you are failed by technology.

11. Ensure that you use Learning Intentions and Success Criteria, even if the school is unfamiliar with them, so you can measure who has made progress in your plenary.

12. Embrace the situation. You do not know the children and they do not know you but there is nothing you can do about that. As long as you deliver a great lesson that keeps them involved and engaged in a spirit of good humour, the children won't forget you and that will become apparent when they speak to the appointment panel after you have left.

Tips for coping in your own environment

If you have been lucky enough to have your teaching assessed in your own classroom, you can at least be confident that you know your classroom environment well enough to perform to the best of your ability. The appointment panel will be expecting you to excel, since they have given you the break of dealing with your everyday working environment. However, do not be lulled into a false sense of security by this and keep in mind the story *The Tortoise and the Hare* from *Aesop's Fables*. Remember 'slow and steady wins the race'.

As confident as you are with your own class and in your own environment, it is easy to assume that:

1. Your class are ready for a lesson of incredulous proportions.

2. Your audience (the appointment panel) will be versed in the nuances of your class and the prior learning that has taken place.

Therefore, it is advisable to proceed with caution before your pride in yourself leads you into a fall of Niagara proportions. To avoid any catastrophic assumptions of either your class or your audience:

1. Take the time to brief your audience on prior learning, SEN and behavioural issues before the lesson takes place.

2. Inform your class that visitors will be coming, because they have heard how good the learning is in their classroom and they want to take some notes.

3. Explain to your class that they will probably ask them questions about the lesson and that they should not be put off by this or worried in any way.

4. Provide the appointment panel with a thorough planning sheet with notes about your expectations for the lesson, including how you will respond to the learning.

5. Teach a lesson that is a continuation of prior learning, rather than assume that the class can respond to something new and unusual.

6. Continue your usual teaching style. Do not be tempted to change for the sake of your audience (slow and steady, etc.).

In this situation, the appointment panel wants to see you in your everyday environment and whilst you may feel that you and your class are ready to try something completely different, do not be tempted. You might be in the middle of a tiresome week of fractions or persuasive texts, but that is genuinely what our job is about at times, so embrace the fact that that is where you are at and teach as you would ordinarily do so. It is what the assessors want to see. If you do attempt something new, it will be obvious and, as a result, you will not be able to express who you really are as a teacher. You will be observed on your personality traits as much as on your teaching abilities, so stick to the norm. Your everyday teaching style, personality and relationship with your class will speak for itself so if you cloud it with irregularity, you will not be presenting yourself in your best light. Be proud of your uniqueness and your own personal style, since it is this that will win you the job, not your ability to create a one-off that may backfire. Remember, slow and steady wins the race!

A final tip

It may be common sense, but a good final tip is to revise everything you know about the Ofsted grade criteria for lessons. You will, no doubt, have been monitored throughout your career and given a variety of judgements, but since you will be judged against current Ofsted criteria, it makes sense that you should try to include as many of their features as possible in your observed lesson.

Obviously you will aim to deliver an outstanding lesson or, at the very least, a good lesson with outstanding features, so let us take a look at what each of these judgements actually mean in terms of the observed lesson you are going to teach.

In an outstanding lesson:

> *'Teaching is at least good and much is outstanding, with the result that the pupils are making exceptional progress. It is highly effective in inspiring pupils and ensuring that they learn extremely well. Excellent subject knowledge is applied consistently to challenge and inspire pupils. Resources, including new technology, make a marked contribution to the quality of learning, as does the precisely targeted support provided by other adults. Teachers and other adults are acutely aware of their pupils' capabilities and of their prior learning*

and understanding, and plan very effectively to build on these. Marking and dialogue between teachers, other adults and pupils are consistently of a very high quality. Pupils understand in detail how to improve their work and are consistently supported in doing so. Teachers systematically and effectively check pupils' understanding throughout lessons, anticipating where they may need to intervene and doing so with striking impact on the quality of learning.'

Ofsted school inspection and lesson observation criteria, updated June 2010

In a good lesson:

'The teaching is consistently effective in ensuring that pupils are motivated and engaged. The great majority of teaching is securing good progress and learning. Teachers generally have strong subject knowledge which enthuses and challenges most pupils and contributes to their good progress. Good and imaginative use is made of resources, including new technology to enhance learning. Other adults' support is well focused and makes a significant contribution to the quality of learning. As a result of good assessment procedures, teachers and other adults plan well to meet the needs of all pupils. Pupils are provided with detailed feedback, both orally and through marking. They know how well they have done and can discuss what they need to do to sustain good progress. Teachers listen to, observe and question groups of pupils during lessons in order to reshape tasks and explanations to improve learning.'

Ofsted school inspection and lesson observation criteria, updated June 2010

Now that you know the criteria, relate it to your class, or the lesson you are planning to teach your unknown class. Plan it out at each point and ensure that you are providing as many of the features as possible that will engage your learners and help them to make the necessary progress. It isn't rocket science, unless that's what you're teaching!

The presentation

Depending on the job you are going for, you may be asked to prepare and deliver a presentation on an area that the school is trying to develop and which will, undoubtedly, play a large part of your new role or in the school in general. In these cases, as sure as salt is salt, you can be certain that it will also play a large part of the selection process.

It may be a rumour that making prisoners of war write and present eloquent, informative and enlightening ten-minute presentations has now become an outlawed practice, but it is still commonly used in educational circles, therefore, the same rules apply, and understandably preparation is king.

The reasons for putting candidates through this are twofold:

1. The appointment panel wants to see that you are experienced, imaginative and would be able to cope with the demands of the job.

2. The appointment panel wants to see how well you present your ideas verbally and how well your messages will be received by the rest of the school.

Knowing this gives you your starting point since it would be foolish to go into such a situation unprepared, but similarly, inexperience will shine through when presentations are put under scrutiny. It is for this reason that presentations should be approached in the same way as writing letters of application by following the mantra as previously discussed:

Understanding   Experience   Contribution

Let us take a standard presentation title, for example, 'The Role of the Subject Coordinator'. A presentation like this doesn't mean the candidate should reel off a standard list of requirements as if they were reading from a book, but the appointment panel will, however, expect the candidate to explain their understanding of the role backed up by their experience and also say how they will apply both experience and understanding to the benefit of the school.

So, since presentation is king, it is down to you to embrace this when preparing yourself for this ordeal. For example, because you have already scrutinised both the person specification and your experience so far, you should be in a position to apply each and every factor of your presentation to the job in hand. You need to give off a confident (not nonchalant) air, so the appointment panel is able to see that you are experienced enough to handle the responsibility as much as you are enthusiastic to grow as a professional, by taking on the new and exciting role that is on offer.

As well as adopting the 'Understanding, Experience and Contribution' approach to your presentation, it is also advisable to couple this with the following approach:

      Strategic   Tactical   Operational

"But hang on there, Mr. Writer, you're bamboozling us with too many tips and strategies in which to succeed", I hear you say! Well, before you throw the book down and stomp off to demand a refund, just hear me out, as it will all make sense in the end.

The 'Strategic, Tactical and Operational' approach is a tried-and-tested means of expressing your understanding of the role on offer. To explain this it would be pertinent for me to say what this actually means.

In management terms, the words 'strategic', 'tactical' and 'operational' are just ways of expressing the different levels of managing your overall vision, or in other words turning your dreams into reality. Strategy involves your overall vision, tactical involves the medium-term methods of getting things done, i.e. the mechanics and systems that you will put into place, and operational merely means how this works on a day-to-day basis.

To expand on this, let's consider baking a birthday cake. The vision (strategy) is that you need a cake for a party and you want to make sure it is greeted with delight and expectation, therefore you will study different types of cake until you are certain you have found one that fulfils all expectations. Next, (tactical) you need to prepare for making a cake that matches your vision so you will begin to gather all of the resources (ingredients and implements) you need to make the vision a reality. Finally, (operational) you will literally follow the instructions using all of the resources you have gathered to make the vision become a physical reality. This is the part of the process where the sleeves are rolled up, actual kneading takes place, the flavour is added and all is put into the oven, or in other words, the bit that gets the vision done.

Now let's refer this back to the original standard presentation title of 'The Role of the Subject Coordinator' and break things down a bit more. Just like baking a cake, the subject you will be coordinating can be approached in the same way. For example:

Strategic

In your presentation, you will need to outline how you see the subject being integrated into the overall running of the school and, in doing so, how this will raise its status with staff. This is your overall vision and should clearly show **understanding** of the subject and similarly your **understanding** of effective subject management. It will be backed up by your research into the school and will take on board both the person specification and the job description.

Tactical

Once you have delivered your strategy to the appointment panel, you will have to follow this up with the mechanisms you will put in place to ensure that this happens. Do you remember the gathering of ingredients and implements? Well, in order to ensure that a subject is coordinated effectively, for example, you will need to have an idea of both staff understanding of the subject (training needs), and the resources the school has that will help to equip staff to deliver it effectively. Therefore, part of your tactics will involve an audit of resources and staff understanding. From here, you will also need to put into place a system of monitoring (teaching and learning), so you can then begin to ascertain what the quality of provision is currently in the school. This, coupled with your provision of exemplary practice for other staff members to observe, will help you to begin writing an action plan for subject development throughout the school. Of course, all of this will be backed up in the presentation by experience of how you have done this before. So, now that you have your **strategy** and your **tactics** in place, clearly demonstrating your **understanding** and **experience**, you can move on to the day-to-day elements of the job in hand.

Operational

Time is tight in schools and, as a result, you need to create maximum effect in the time that is available to you. Therefore, this is your chance to demonstrate that, no matter how grand your plans, you recognise that they are going to be delivered within finite budgets and equally challenging time constraints. However, because you have both experience and understanding, you will now be in a position to demonstrate how your strategy, tactics, understanding and experience will enable you to **contribute** to the development of the school through your **operational** suggestions.

For example, you know that Rome wasn't built in a day, so you will break up your tactics term by term. Here you will demonstrate that in the first term you will begin to build a picture of the subject in the school and the provisions available to you. In the first term you will have monitored teaching and learning, so, you will also be in a position to make suggestions and begin building your resource wish list that will enable your colleagues to achieve your targets of them. You will be wary of expenditure and so will either deliver whole-school training yourself or bring in LEA support to deliver training as required. You will also be able to demonstrate that your clear and defined understanding of the role, based on your experiences, will enable you to identify that the second term will be devoted to staff training, following up your initial observations and use of resources bought, as well as building a timetable for colleagues to observe good practice both in your classroom and those of others around the authority. In the second term you will also bring in support from specialists such as ASTs or LEA consultants to back you up and solidify the expectations.

Finally, in the third term, you will expect to see improvements in both understanding and practice, leading to improved learning amongst pupils. This should be qualified through improved results (which you have been tracking since you took on the role, of course!) and improved teacher confidence. At the end of your third term, you will be in a position to consolidate what has happened throughout the year and will begin enriching it by allowing staff to share their experiences so far and ultimately to begin building a shared action plan for improvement. Seems like a pretty good **contribution** to me! But to clarify the connections between the two approaches, allow me to use a graph:

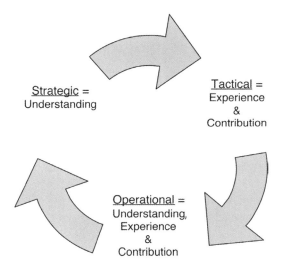

Strategic =
Understanding

Tactical =
Experience
&
Contribution

Operational =
Understanding,
Experience
&
Contribution

This should all lead to a very good presentation indeed that clearly defines how you will help the school to move forward in their chosen area, and if that doesn't work then at least you should have a very nice cake!

Finally, the art of a good presentation is to stick to the script as much as you can. You and I know that you will have been through it a hundred times or more before you actually deliver it, but that doesn't mean that come the moment of delivery, you won't forget everything and fall like jelly into a quivering wreck on the floor. I myself have entered into a couple of presentations and been let down by technology or the small text of my notes. Therefore, a few more tips at this stage won't do any harm:

1. Back up your presentation on two memory sticks to be certain it will be there when you need it.

2. Back it up even further with paper notes as well (just to be on the safe side).

3. Do not be too fancy with PowerPoint and technology as it can bite you on the backside. You may want to enter the room through a rising stage with dry ice and dramatic music, but the panel are more interested in what you have to say rather than how you present it.

4. A good PowerPoint presentation will speak volumes with the fewest of words.

5. Remember to slow down and speak with confidence – clock-watching is inevitable, but use it to your advantage by reaching the end of each point by a certain time.

6. Try to assure and interest the panel with your ideas, using this opportunity to clearly identify your intentions should you be successful. This is usually done by speaking confidently, sticking to your script and not ad-libbing.

7. Be yourself as much as is possible, as the appointment panel is looking for personable qualities as much as professional ones.

On the final point and at the end of all this advice, my final tip is to offer these words of wisdom. Whilst sitting through a selection of unconvincing interviewees when appointing an ICT Coordinator, the final candidate came in to the room, stumbling as she did so and throwing notes and preparations all over the floor. After she had corrected herself, brushed herself down and removed her high heels, she began her presentation with these immortal words:

'Well, that's the ice broken. Let's hope my presentation goes better!'

I knew straightaway that she was someone I could work with.

The interview

The application form and letter are written, the interview request has been responded to, the presentation is over and now the final hurdle awaits you – a gruelling thirty-minute (and very often longer) question-and-answer session known as the interview.

Some of you may tremble at the thought of it whereas others may just stop reading right here, throw the book away and open a bottle of wine whilst declaring to yourself how stupid you were in the first place for even thinking about moving on. Whatever your reaction to the thought of attending an interview, spare a thought for those on the other side. (Hear me out on this one!) I have sat through a variety of interviews, both as the candidate and as a member of the appointment team, and whilst it is obviously worse on your side, the panel have probably sat through a range of presentations and interviews before and heard longwinded, elaborate and stunted answers, as well as had to scribble notes down and fill in the tick boxes at the same time. Then, once the last candidate has left for the day, their job is not over, since they still have to tot up the scores and discuss the various merits (or not) of the different candidates and then finally make a considered decision. Not until the references have been read and the final nod is given can they go home for their tea!

I know what you are thinking. As you contemplate the thought of answering to the Spanish Inquisition, it might be difficult for you to consider your audience, but it would probably be the most important thing that you could do at this stage. You need to stand out for all the right reasons and even though you have given a blinding presentation already, you can still falter at the final stage, so you need to consider how you will hit the right points knowledgeably and succinctly, whilst maintaining your

sense of personality and humour – that is what will single you out from the other candidates. Easy then!

Before we deal with the questions the appointment panel might ask you, let us start at the beginning and consider the basics.

Presentation

Obviously it is ill-advised to wear jeans and a T-shirt, even if that would put you at ease, but just exactly how should you present yourself? It is quite true that people make first impressions in the first thirty seconds of meeting you, so standard formal attire is advisable. Do not be tempted to wear clothes that are going to make you feel more uncomfortable than you already do, such as incredibly high heels or a stuffy suit, as this will put you at a disadvantage straight away. Instead, opt for your most presentable and professional clothes, preferably ones that you have worn before. To put this simply, don't buy new shoes! You will be conscious of them, they may rub and it always feels awkward wearing them for the first time! You need to feel as comfortable as possible when you walk into that room, so do everything you can to enable you to do so.

Presentation is not just about how you look. It is also about how you present yourself socially. Walk in with a big smile and wait to be introduced and invited to sit down before doing so. These are just basic manners, but it shows you have an appreciation of your place in this particular situation.

You will probably be introduced to the chair of governors since they will have the overall responsibility for leading events. Should you be applying for a less senior promotion, you may be introduced initially by the headteacher, with other members of the governing body present, but no matter who it is, make sure that you wait to be greeted before launching in with your hand to the first person you see as you walk through the door.

If you are more comfortable speaking with your jacket off, then ask politely if they would mind if you took it off. Again, this shows an understanding of protocol. There will, inevitably, be some small talk before the interview begins and you get settled down, therefore engage with it politely but do not be tempted to relax into colloquial banter or say too much, as this will portray your nerves or may suggest that you are overconfident and see the interview as a formality. Politeness is key, so make sure that you are ready to manage the situation as it occurs.

So, you are seated, your jacket is off and your shoes are shiny. You have shaken hands (firmly but not aggressively) and discussed the weather, so there is nothing left for you to do other than brace yourself for question number one.

Answering questions – part 1

Your interviewing panel will, invariably, be made up of the headteacher, members of the governing body, a representative from the LEA and, possibly, another member of the senior management team. Each member of the panel will have a couple of questions based on their particular section of the person specification, so, for example, a parent governor will probably ask you a question relating to your understanding of community cohesion for their first question or the SMT member may ask you a question surrounding classroom management. Each member of the panel will ask you one question and then move on to the next member and so on. You can usually expect about ten questions, each with direct reference to the person specification and they will be worded in such a way that you will need to pick out the underlying theme first and then go on to answer, highlighting your **understanding**, **experience** and ability to **contribute** to the school.

The first question will probably be a warm-up question that will allow you to demonstrate something positive from your career, designed, ultimately, to put you at ease. Examples of these types of question might be:

- Share with us an experience from your career that has made you particularly proud.

- What has been the most rewarding experience you have had in teaching and why was it so rewarding?

- What would be your ideal environment for learning and how would you develop it?

- What do you think makes a good manager?

When you look at questions like these written down it seems totally innocuous, but many times I have seen candidates bamboozled by them since they are so tense and expecting intensive scrutiny from the offset.

In truth, questions like these can have a hidden agenda, so be prepared to answer using all of the skills you have mustered so far. Let us take the first question as an example.

'Share with us an experience from your career that has made you particularly proud.'

Firstly, do not be tempted to relay an extensive account of exactly what you did, who was involved and the various traumas you went through to achieve your success in the first place. Rather, use the skill of succinctness to get the point across. Try to keep all of your answers down to around two to three minutes in length and if you are not certain that you have answered the question well enough, you can always call on the trick of 'getting them to tell you what they're looking for', but more about that later. In this instance a well-rounded and succinct answer will be:

Understanding – *Teaching is about enabling children to learn through support, encouragement and dedication. With that in mind I would say something I'm particularly proud of are the learning achievements made by a middle ability group that were finding new work difficult to grasp in Numeracy.*

Experience – *First, I held individual pupil interviews with the children, coupled with simple assessments to try and get to the bottom of their learning gaps. This helped me to write individual education plans for them and, equally, to plan a series of teacher-led group sessions that catered for the gaps and helped them to catch up. Finally, I worked closely with their parents and set up a series of homework challenges that complemented the work they were doing in class. The improvement in their results at the end of the term was marked and I was particularly proud when I saw that the hands of this particular group were going up more frequently in whole-class sessions and their overall confidence in maths growing.*

Contribution – *I would like to bring this sense of supportive teaching to St Anywhere Primary School should I be successful. I would work closely with the assessment coordinator to ensure that underachieving pupils were singled out and appropriate interventions were put in place. I would also like to strengthen links with parents in this way.*

Answers that follow the same pattern as the application form and presentation will highlight all of your strengths consistently and will cement any initial thoughts about your application in the minds of the panel. By avoiding telling funny tales or going all around the houses when giving your reply and sticking to the key points, your answers will always be succinct, relevant and informative.

Answering questions – part 2

Just like the first question, the rest of the questions you can expect to receive need to be answered in the same three-part manner as a means of getting your points across concisely and thoroughly. As soon as you hear the question, reflect on it. (Ask the panel member to repeat it if you are uncertain of what they said.) Then consider how you can best start your answer in a way that shows understanding of the key underlying theme. Once you have begun showing your understanding, this will trigger an experience you can divulge and, ultimately, will lead you to say how you will further develop these main concepts at their school.

In many ways, it is this element of your answers that will be of most interest, particularly to the headteacher, since it will show that you have an understanding of the current status of the school based on your research before the interview. Whilst you don't want to recite chapter and verse of the Ofsted report itself, you can refer to both that and other pieces of pertinent information you received in the application pack to show that you are motivated and knowledgeable about the school.

You don't even need to be so explicit as to mention the Ofsted report itself, but you can ensure that your answers lean towards the main findings of the report in the final part of your answers. This will raise eyebrows amongst the panel and will certainly tick boxes when it comes to showing how you will fit into the overall development of the school, so don't be afraid to err towards it in the final parts of your answers.

Remember that the questions you receive will generally be pertinent to the particular member of the panel who is asking, for example:

- The headteacher and SMT member are likely to ask questions about the main responsibilities of the job, working in a team, behaviour management, etc.

- The LEA representative is likely to ask questions about teaching and learning, classroom environment, assessment, etc.

- The chair of governors is likely to ask questions about the whole-school ethos, personal qualities, whole-school development, etc.

- The parent governor is likely to ask questions about community cohesion, working with parents, utilising the wider community, etc.

The key point is to be prepared and to have read the job description, person specification, information about the school and the Ofsted report as thoroughly as possible, so you will have had a chance to prepare some answers in advance. It is a bad idea to learn answers off by heart and then try to make them fit the question, since this can make you very uncomfortable as you wrestle with ways to make them relevant. It is far better to prepare some good examples based on each element of the person specification, so should a question come based on some of the key points, you will be prepared for it and can demonstrate your experience with confidence.

In all honesty, you can never truly predict exactly what you will be asked or how it will be worded, but by reading through the person specification, etc. you can roughly predict the general areas that will be visited and, as such, should be prepared enough to give thorough, well-rounded answers that demonstrate why you are the best candidate for the position.

The old 'getting them to tell you what they're looking for' trick

I first came upon this chestnut when I was interviewing a young teacher for a promotion at my school. When asked the question 'Define a good learning environment for children', she went on to describe how children learn and how, in the past, she had set up environments for learning. On the whole it wasn't a bad answer and I could glean from it what I could expect if she were appointed. At the end of the answer, however, she asked

'Does that answer your question or would you like me to elaborate further?'

Rather taken aback by this response, I **was** in fact interested to know more about her working practice and so asked her to elaborate a little more on how she incorporated teaching assistants into her classroom routine. This immediately gave the candidate another shot at the same question, but this time she embellished her answer with all of the information I required and more about her working practice in general and how it had led to improvements at the school.

This was the only time she used this trick and it was after an answer that she was unsure about, but she used it well and, yes, of course, she went on to get the job! I asked her later where she had got the idea from and she told me that her father was a management consultant who had given her a variety of tricks of the trade before the interview. Very good!

I have seen similar tricks used and, yes, of course, I have used a variety of them myself. Similar questions used to get the interviewing panel to open up include:

'Have I answered the question thoroughly enough?'

'Is that the answer you were looking for?'

'Is this a question about...?'

And so on. Obviously, an interviewing panel does not have to respond to your questions, but if asked with the appropriate amount of humility, manners and professionalism, it is surprising how you can sway an interviewer into helping you to improve your answers by giving you the time to do so. Use them with caution though as you do not want to blow your chances before you have taken them.

Success and failure at interview

The fact of the matter is, you have more chance of being unsuccessful at interview than you do of succeeding, but that does not mean that you should assume failure before you begin. To some degree, this is why the whole experience can be so stressful in the first place. You are presenting yourself to be judged by a group of strangers and this is where feelings of anxiety are born. It is very easy to question whether you are, in fact, ready to take the plunge and to presume that all of your answers will be woefully inadequate on the day or that your presentation will be so wide of the mark as to render it worthless. This is because, in many ways, you are dealing with an unknown quantity and that, in itself, leads to uncertainty and, of course, leads you to question yourself relentlessly. The way around this though, as we have discovered already, is to make the unknown more familiar by doing your homework on the school and, equally, on yourself.

You do not want to come across as overconfident, nor do you want to appear meek, so on top of the anxieties of how you will answer the questions themselves, you also have to concern yourself with how you are perceived by the panel. It is very easy to overinflate the importance of the situation as well. I know myself that I have worried myself into sleepless nights over interviews in the past, only to kick myself the next day when I looked tired and dishevelled and my answers were fuzzy because I was so tired I could not concentrate.

Feedback

At the end of the process, the chair of governors or the headteacher will contact you to let you know the news. If you have been unsuccessful, then this will be your chance to get feedback on your performance and, of course, to learn from the experience. You may not get feedback right away, but you will be given a time when the designated person will be able to go over your interview and presentation in more detail. This is usually because it will be the end of an extraordinarily long day for the interviewing panel and, like you, they will need time to reflect on your performance and collate their notes. I advise any unsuccessful candidate to get their feedback, even if they may never want to think about the interview again, because it is extremely valuable and, of course, will give you vital information that will help you in the future.

Whatever the news, however, when you receive the post-interview telephone call, be professional and diligent, since, if you were unsuccessful you may be applying to that authority in the future and will want them to have a good impression of you none-theless. And if you were successful, you don't want them to question their decision from the offset!

So, in a nutshell...

When all is said and done, interviews and the whole application process are just a barrier that you must get through in order to achieve what you know you are capable of in the future. You have already been successful in the past or else you would not be in a position to apply for a promotion in the first place, so draw on the fact that you have been through all of this before and that this time you were the one that ticked all of the boxes. Remember that on that occasion, there were unsuccessful candidates on the day who, when receiving the news, will have questioned themselves relentlessly. No doubt they went on to achieve the position they wanted in the future.

If you are successful, then you will deserve to give yourself a pat on the back because all of the hard work and effort you put in from the very beginning will have paid off. However, if you are unsuccessful, rather than beating yourself up about it, use the experience positively to learn from, safe in the knowledge that eventually you will land the job you want. Every time you are unsuccessful, you will gain experience of the process that will enable you to approach the next interview more confidently. The premise of application and preparation will always remain the same, as will the tactics you adopt, and eventually the job will be yours. Either way, successful or not, you will have put in the effort and it is that that is your most resounding victory.

As Kipling tells us, success is when

> _'you can meet with triumph and disaster and treat those two imposters just the same...'_

Section 3: The next step

You got it, so now what?

Leaving your current school

Starting at your new school

Presenting yourself to your new colleagues

You can't change the world overnight but you need to make a start

Internal promotions

The future

So, in a nutshell...

You got it, so now what?

So, you planned, studied, prepared and performed, and when the telephone call came, it was good news. The party is over, the leaving cards and gifts from school are safely packed away and the day has come – your new job awaits you. So, now what?

Firstly, once you are successful, there is a certain amount of transition that needs to take place before you start. You will have opportunities to visit the new school and begin setting out your stall, but don't be too quick to get started. Starting at a new school takes a period of adjustment for all concerned to get to know each other. Starting your first day by giving staff a pile of extra work is not going to make you any friends very quickly and will put you in danger of being labelled as a headteacher's stooge. This is your time and your opportunity to make your dreams a professional reality, so why rush? You need to consider exactly how you want to be perceived by your new colleagues, as much as you did by the interviewing panel who appointed you.

Leaving your current school

Another important element of receiving a promotion, is that you will, at some point, have to leave your current school. This needs to be done with the same amount of professionalism and grace you will be showing your new employers and colleagues. You may have worked there for a long time, or only for a couple of years, but either way, you need to leave the school making sure you have done everything possible to support the new staff member who will be taking over from you and, similarly, that you have thanked everyone concerned who has helped you to grow along the way.

It is both personally and professionally proper to thank your colleagues for their support, etc. and also to thank the children and parents as well. Remember that you will have grown as a result of working there and that is something that needs to be appreciated. The school took a chance on you, nurtured your abilities and developed you professionally along the way. You are, therefore, in a position to take on your new role at your new school, because of the work you did at the old, so as much as you have worked incredibly hard to get where you have, some appreciation needs to be given to those around you. It is well advised to never leave a workplace under a cloud, but to ensure that your exit is positive and you are well thought of. As the old saying goes 'Be good to those on the way up as you don't know if you will see them on the way down!'

Starting at your new school

I have seen countless colleagues make the mistake of 'hitting the ground running' and assuming that everyone in the school has their enthusiasm and understanding of the job in hand, because they don't. Think of your old school and the variety of different personalities you may have met there. How you dealt with and worked with them was entirely built on a sense of experience and understanding of them as people and professionals and that, of course, takes time to build up.

A good tip is to have a plan of how you intend to set about fulfilling your new role that has been agreed by your new headteacher and stick to it. The best changes, and certainly the ones that have the most long-lasting effects, are the ones that are integrated slowly but consistently, relying on consultation and discussion. This ensures that there is a shared sense of understanding from which to build the changes you want to introduce. It is far easier to achieve successful change in a school if staff have been allowed to contribute to the changes rather than have them forced upon them. Even if you are ready to get stuck in, your colleagues might not be there just yet, so rather than make your job more difficult by alienating yourself, make it easier by winning new colleagues around and actually getting to know them. Apart from your family, you spend more time with your professional colleagues than anyone else, so it kind of helps if you like each other, doesn't it?

Presenting yourself to your new colleagues

Remember when you were an NQT and you walked into the staffroom on the first day? Scary, wasn't it? But this was made less so by the sympathetic welcome you were given. Well, this is similar but not the same because you no longer have the sympathy of all teachers who have been through their own NQT experiences. This time you are an experienced teacher charged with making a difference in the school and that means that the way you need to approach your first day is entirely different. Your colleagues will initially judge you based on the fact that you have been chosen because you were thought the most likely person to implement changes and this will slightly taint their initial welcomes. Don't get me wrong, this doesn't mean that you will be professionally shunned, or worse, ostracised completely, but it does mean that emotions may be flying high. Perhaps you are replacing someone who was particularly popular or maybe you are the replacement for someone who had been through the competence and capability procedure. Either way, you are the person who is going to change things at the school and as we all know, change doesn't sit with some as well as it does with others. It is for this reason that your first few days at the school need to be treated with a definite approach that will ensure that your colleagues see you as a person first and a professional second.

You know how to teach well and how good schools function, but do not assume that just because you knew your old school inside out that this one will be the same. Yes, there will be elements that are similar, such as similar resources and planning pro-formas, etc. but this school is completely different to your old one in many different ways, and that is exactly how it should be. Schools, like people, have individual personalities that have been shaped by their experience and changes that have occurred throughout their lives. There will be some staff there who may have seen a variety of staff come and go and, likewise, there may be staff who are less experienced than you. No matter who they are though, the one thing that all of your new colleagues have over you is experience of the school they work in and you, like it or not, don't.

Your new staff will, undoubtedly, want to tell you all about the school's history as well as its problems in a bid to get to know you. They will also fill you in on certain families, mistakes that have been made and what to look out for, and as much as you want to fit in to your new environment quickly and make a good impression, the best thing that you can do is to remain appreciative, polite and at all times professional. You don't want to make 'friends' too quickly, nor do you want be stand-offish or rude. You need to be appreciative of the fact that your colleagues are welcoming, but focus your energies and attention on getting established in your classroom or office. Asking questions when they arise to the right people will tell you a lot about them quickly, so just spend your first few days getting to know your environment and building relationships with those more experienced about the school than you.

You also need to build relationships with the SMT and, in particular, the headteacher, since that is who first took a chance on you; you don't want to let them down. Finding time to spend with your new boss will be time very well spent and will give you an opportunity to discuss your plans for implementing your job description in the context of whole-school development. Your headteacher will see the overall picture of the school and whilst your role is to develop one or two particular parts of it, it is their role to support you as you do it and fit your work into the school's other areas for development.

You can't change the world overnight but you need to make a start

As keen as you will undoubtedly be to start building Rome, taking time to discuss your plans with your headteacher will ensure that your thoughts are focused and your energies are not wasted. Your headteacher will guide you as to their expectations of you and the role, how much meeting time, etc. will be devoted to your role, your budget, release time and overall time scale. You need to have an idea about how you see your particular area developing, and how fast, but be prepared to have some of your plans put on hold for the time being. A good headteacher knows that you will need to get to know both the school and its people before you can begin to make the progress you will, undoubtedly, be desperate to. You need to audit before you can do anything of real value, so focus on this above everything else at first – this and establishing yourself in the school. You are part of the school's overall development and, as such, you need to be aware that whilst it is important that the school, through your work, develops in the right direction, it is also important that you become a trusted member of staff with professional credibility to boot and that will only come from the hard work you put into the everyday part of your new role – teaching and learning.

If this is your first promotion with new responsibilities, it can sometimes come as a bit of a shock when you realise that you are now juggling everything that involves good teaching and learning, classroom management and supporting a whole-school ethos, as well as the leadership and development of a particular area of the school.

Firstly, if you find yourself in this situation, don't panic! As I mentioned earlier, a good headteacher will make sure that you have the time to settle into the routines of the school before you start to make any significant progress with your management role, so relax into the role and put your stamp on the school in the classroom. You are an experienced and dedicated professional who has learnt some very valuable lessons along the way, so take some solace in the fact that you know you are capable of performing well in the classroom and impacting on the lives of the children you teach. This will ultimately give you confidence and, similarly, will show others that you are competent and capable. If you have done things a certain way in your old school, then begin to bring some of these qualities to the new, but be careful as this is not your opportunity to change the entire working practice of the school. You may feel horrified at how some things are done or, similarly, you may think that some practice in the school could be modified to serve your needs, but once again, caution is advised. Perhaps in your old school you did things differently, but that came about over time and through professional discourse. You may know the successes your old working practice may have brought, but you also know the time it took to realise that success, so do not try and change things to suit you. This is a mistake that is very often made and can lead to alienation very quickly.

You are new to the school and you need to 'fit in' at first. Make the best of what you have got and ensure that you fit in to their working practice and not the other way around. This way, by working within the parameters you have been given, you will be certain that your work will be measured and judged by what you do. If problems are obvious, then you will only be able to make changes when you have shown that you have tried to work with them. As a result, if you do want to introduce changes to everyday working practice in the school, it will be based on your experience, rather than a quick judgement.

Remember, every school is different and what works well in one will not necessarily work as well in another. Bide your time before changing the world, as it will serve you better in the long run.

Internal promotions

You may have applied for an internal promotion, meaning that whilst you are already known within the school and have grown and learnt within it, your position in the general running of things has changed. Now, you are a member of the team who is pushing the school forward rather than facilitating the change. This is one of the most significantly difficult professional changes to manage, since where you were once one of the team, you are now a leader, meaning people's perceptions of you will change very quickly.

The main reason for this is because there is a distinct difference between the role of a class teacher and a senior leader, but this is not necessarily a bad thing. There should be a difference between the two, since a leader has been given an expectation to make a change and lead other staff into changing their practice to show cohesion for the good of all at the school. However, what if your staff know too much about you or, perhaps, have seen a side of you that you would rather they had not? You now have to change people's perceptions of you and show that you are a leader of people. You can only do this by changing their outward perceptions of you by rising to the challenge. But how?

Well, in many ways, whilst this type of promotion is one of the more difficult ones, it can also be made slightly easier by the fact that you also know as much about your colleagues as they do about you. Therefore, you know which colleagues will be more likely to bad-mouth the management and any new initiative they introduce. Similarly, you will know the colleagues who will be more likely to go with new strategies and make them a part of their working practice. You also know the school and all who sail in it, meaning that you know the children, families and governors. Whilst this may increase the pressure somewhat, you need to use it to your advantage, increasing your chances of succeeding in your role by capitalising on the knowledge you have.

My main tips for such promotions are:

- Go slowly, but not too slowly since you have already built up an in-depth understanding of the school.

- Audit, audit, audit. This will increase your knowledge of practice around the school and will highlight the areas for development.

- Change your status, not by becoming Mr or Mrs Manager overnight, but by working into the role. This can be done by challenging inappropriate behaviour towards you, having high expectations of both yourself and of your colleagues, but also by working with the rhythm of the school that you know so well.

- Do not praise publicly but privately. This way you will not come across as patronising or above your station.

- Rise to the challenge and be courageous – it will only go wrong if you allow it to.

You will have the full support of your headteacher and SMT, so use it. Things can change quite quickly in a school, including staff, so by doing a thorough job and making small changes often, you will soon grow into your new role, as difficult as it may seem at first.

The future

You have done what you set out to do and landed your dream job. You are also making good progress in implementing changes and managing the processes involved in change. Make the most of what you are achieving and also make notes, because what you are doing now will, undoubtedly, help you to make further progress throughout your career in the future when you will set about going through the whole application process once more.

Do not be in a rush to go for further promotions too soon. See your new job through to its natural conclusion, since that is what is expected of you and you will not be able to talk about your successes confidently unless you truly do. It does not look great on application forms either when a prospective candidate's employment history shows them flitting from one job to the next with only a year's experience at each one.

Do, however, keep one eye on the future. There is nothing wrong with keeping yourself abreast of current climates and changes. This shows professional enthusiasm and interest. You can do this whilst, all the time, keeping your watchful eye on your current position and the jobs that need to be done. Your confidence levels will, of course, be higher next time around, because not only did you get your current job, you have been successful whilst implementing its job description.

So, in a nutshell...

There are two parts to consider when taking on a new role – leaving and starting – with both being as important as each other. The best way to put this to newly promoted teachers is to end a job as you would like to be remembered and to start one in the same way; that way you will always be thought of as a consummate professional and a thoroughly nice person.

It is never easy starting a new position because there is so much that you want to do in a short time, but by taking your time, finding your feet and establishing yourself in the way you would like to be perceived, you will make a good impression from the offset and before you know it, it will be half term, you will have built a rapport with both children and colleagues, and your first audit will be well underway. After that, the rest will come easy!

If it has taken you some time to get the promotion you wanted, then it will be so much sweeter when the time comes and more reason for you to work hard to set off on the right foot. If you are unsure about how to do that, then put yourself in the shoes of a child starting on their first day in a new school. At first they are shy and uncertain, but with a little encouragement, they soon start to show themselves and before long they are very much a part of the class. In your case, the encourager will be your headteacher and like the new child, if you take the encouragement and be true to your personality, educational beliefs and experience, before long you will become very much a part of the school.

Conclusion

Applying for a promotion is a long, time-consuming and often heartbreaking experience that many people go through every year. Each term as resignation dates get closer, teachers and managers find themselves daring to dream and setting forward on the arduous journey ahead, and for every job application that is submitted, so is a little bit of hope and self-belief.

I now look on the process as a positive one, reading applications with interest rather than dread, and writing my own in a way that I know will emphasise the best points of my experience and pedagogy in a way that is informative and easy to digest.

Reading this, you may have had positive or negative experiences of the process so far, but no matter what they are, you should have learnt something from it that will help you the next time you apply for a promotion.

So, if you got the job, well done, and I hope it promises to be all you hoped for, but if you didn't get it, don't beat yourself up. It wasn't your time, but that time will come.